# Do Something Now!

**be the one who makes something happen**

Rick —
Cheers to being
the Best &
making a difference
DSN ..

For multiple copies and bulk orders, please contact our office

**T: 619.624.9691 / E: info@freibergs.com**

# Praise for Do Something Now!

**Get Off The Log!** Three frogs sat on a log at the edge of the swamp. One decided to jump in. How many frogs are still on the log? Nope! There are still three. Deciding and doing are not the same. Progress, success and growth are all the result of execution, not dreaming, planning or deciding. And, *Do Something Now* by the prolific and provocative Freibergs will give you and your organization the courage and capacity to get off the log! Read this excellent book and turn great intentions into productive results.

**Chip R. Bell**, Bestselling Author and Customer Loyalty Guru

**I AM DOING SOMETHING RIGHT NOW!** I am a venture capitalist. I don't give a 5 star out easily and certainly it is very hard to convince a guy who has built and invested in so many companies that your ideas are better or cleaner or will make a difference. I would get this book fast, especially for entire companies. *DO SOMETHING NOW* shows us how to unlock the potential of personal innovation and how to harness it into actionable and accountable results.

**Billy Glynn**, CEO, Brand Equity, Inc.

**Take Action!** As a leader who is passionate about bringing out the best in people and organizations, I am amazed by how often the best results are held back by one simple thing: The failure to act. *Do Something Now* shows us how to fight through the things that hold us back from achieving greatness as individuals, teams, and businesses. This simple blueprint empowers us to create more fulfilling lives and more successful businesses by inspiring us to take action and DO SOMETHING NOW!

**Sheldon Harris**, CEO, Complete Nutrition, Co-Founder, Cold Stone Creamery

**The Freibergs Have Done It Again!** *Do Something Now!* is fast-paced, creative, and inspiring, the sort of book that is hard to put down. With thought-provoking insights, first-hand accounts of leadership lessons from the likes of Southwest Airlines and Tata, and videos from the authors, this is a very innovative publication from two leaders in the field of innovation.

**John W. Gates**, Senior Partner, Avion Consulting Group

***Do Something Now*** will re-engage people, challenge them to innovate and empower them to be more accountable for leading change. Read and share! This book calls people to give it a shot, dare to try, and turn ideas into innovations.

**Chad Linebaugh**, General Manager, Sundance Mountain Resort

**The Permission Slip We All Need.** Taking action leads to learning, invention and ultimately progress. The solution, the resources and the path are rarely visible at the onset of any initiative that breaks through business as usual. If you want to make a difference you have to make something happen. I'll personally refer to *Do Something Now* often for a daily dose of inspiration with a shot of whoop ass!

**Greg A. Ray**, CFO, Brand Equity, Inc

**Here they go again!** If you know the Freibergs, this book makes sense. If you don't, then get off your butt and find out what they have to say about getting things done, empowering yourself to be a winner, or leading the change you always say needs to occur! If you don't lead, your complaints about others' inaction have no validity. This book will give you the inspiration to start and the tenacity to FINISH the job effectively.

**Jeffrey R. Bowman**, Former Fire Chief, City of San Diego

***Do Something Now*** inspires it's readers to action by encouraging self-empowerment in everything they do, from the big to the small. Learn how you can encourage a culture of Doing Something Now. So, what should you do now? Read and then share this book.

**Peter Stark**, CEO, PBS Company

***Do Something Now* inspires the innovator in all of us.** In a market where new players are entering the game every day, innovation and creative thinking are critical to success. This call to action must be shared with everyone in your organization. Seeds of ideas can come from all corners of an organization. This book teaches you how to nurture those seeds and turn unexpected ideas into innovations and improvements. *Do Something Now* will re-engage, empower and motivate you to innovate. If you don't, someone else will!

**Czar Johnson**, Director of Mountain Operations, Sundance Resort

**You can change your life...right now!** This is just the book I needed to catapult me into a higher performance orbit by empowering me to 'just do it'. At this time of my life I needed an external force to help me unleash my full potential...'Do Something Now' just came into my life at the right time. This book challenged me and dared me to go ahead and actually try out my wild ideas. The self-empowerment has invigorated my entire life. I've changed....forever.

**Jagdeesh Shivdasani**, Head of Business Development at Rinira Technologies Pvt. Ltd.

**Great way to re-energize the "doer" in us all**. What a great read. Sometimes we just need to be reminded and guided to be accountable and lead the changes we want to see happen. Love DSN as a way of life!

**Jen Arricale,** World Champion Body Builder

**Assigned book to my Executive MBA class**. With over 30 years experience teaching innovation and consulting with leaders of high-technology companies, I think the Freibergs have nailed the single most important answer to every company's questions about innovation: do something now! The strength of the book is the case it makes for the strategic advantages associated with an organizational bias toward action.

I am so impressed with the book and what it adds to the existing literature on innovation that I am assigning it to my *Leading Innovation* Executive MBA course. If our executives truly intend to lead innovation, *Do Something Now* needs to be part of their skill set.

**Jack W Brittain**, Pierre Lassonde Presidential Chair, David Eccles School of Business, University of Utah

**Great book!** I am a small business owner. Honestly, I don't read many business books. I am overwhelmed with changes I know I should make to my business without overwhelming myself by adding a pile of new ones. I make an exception when the Freibergs pen a new book. Their books read more like novels with life lessons. Highly recommend anything they write!

**Dan Haggerty** Owner/Entrepreneur, Haggerty's Music

**I'm Doing Something.** As an owner of a small business in a constantly changing field, the tendency is to sit, wait, watch and react...and always end up three steps behind. Reading the Freiberg's books always energizes me to try and be on the forefront rather than reacting. I loved it!

**Jeff Katz**, CEO, Katz Architecture

# Do Something Now!

**be the one who makes something happen**

**Dr. Kevin and Dr. Jackie Freiberg**

Co-authors of the international Best-seller NUTS! Southwest Airlines' Crazy Recipe for Business and Personal Success, GUTS!, BOOM!, and NANOVATION: How a Little Car Can Teach the World to Think Big and Act Bold

Published by freibergs.com, a San Diego Consulting Group, Inc. company and CreateSpace.com 

ISBN-13: 978-1499546088

ISBN-10: 1499546084

Design and eBook conversion by: Reality Premedia Services Pvt. Ltd., Pune, India

# Dedication

## To the dreamers in search of doers

May this book be the nudge you need to START, to look around, reach out, partner, collaborate and hold yourself accountable to bringing great ideas and dormant dreams to life!

We thank Patti Cipro, our COO (Chief Optimism Officer) recently promoted to Chief DSN Officer. Patti's remarkable and unending reserve of optimism helped bring this book to print.

Patti, you are an inspiring example of what it takes to Do Something Now!, we are blessed by your CAN DO spirit and grateful for the gifts you bring to our team.

# QR Codes

Here is your first chance to **Do Something Now!**

If you are unfamiliar, a QR Code or **Quick Response Code** is a two-dimensional barcode that can be read using smartphone applications and dedicated QR reading devices. A QR code links directly to videos, emails, websites, phone numbers, text, and more.

You will find many QR codes in this book, so let's get started! Do Something Now, go to the App store and download a QR Code reader. There are many to choose from, here are a few options:

Barcode Scanner

Zapper

NeoReader

Kaywa

freibergs.com

# Table of Contents

# Do Something Now!

**Three simple letters.**
**Three simple words that could change your organization—maybe even your life.**

DSN The difference between those who give history a shove and those who wished they had made a difference.

DSN The difference between those who get to the future first and those who are forced to play catch-up.

DSN The difference between those who make the rules and those forced to play by the rules others establish.

DSN The difference between vibrant, growing organizations and the ones that are stuck.

DSN The difference between living life intentionally and watching life just happen.

DSN The difference between those who are afraid of regret and those who are afraid of failure.

DSN The difference between nothing special and being indispensable.

Our lives begin to
end the day we
become silent about things
that matter.

Martin Luther King Jr.

# Player or Spectator?

In the game of life, there are players and those who shrink from their God-given abilities. Players charge on to the field with passion, energy, and a desire to win—sometimes they get their hands dirty, their faces sweaty, and their bodies bloody and bruised by giving their all to the game.

Spectating, on the other hand, is easy. No risk. No skin in the game. It's much easier to sit around and intellectualize, debate the merits of a new idea, gather more data, buy new technology, and revise the plan than it is to make something happen.

Spectators are comfortable sitting in the stands, criticizing plays and heading for the door in the second half when success eludes the team or the show doesn't entertain.

Spectators do a lot of talking, but talking is not doing. Discussing an idea, writing a report or giving a presentation is not the same as DSN.

Of course the problem with this cultural norm is that it creeps into our organizations. We are told to watch; not lead, and consume; not create. Innovation requires players. To be a player is to have a VOICE, to have influence. It is to speak up and shape policies and practices that make someone's world better. To poke a finger in the eye of the status quo.

### Players want to be the CAUSE; not the EFFECT.

To be the cause of something is to "put it out there," to put a stake in the ground. To be the effect is to passively live with it—accept it as it is. Players want to influence the outcome of the game.

There's always a cost to being a player. You will encounter the soothsayers and cynics and spectators who tell you that you're naive, that you're too idealistic.

### Players look obstacles in the eye and say, "GAME ON!"

So, decide what you want to accomplish. Determine what price you are willing to pay for it. Ask yourself, "What am I willing to stand up for, bleed for and commit to?"

### Because *that's* what is going to actually get done.

Your **spouse,**
your **children,**
your **boss,**
your **co-workers** and
your **customers**

don't care about what

you intend to do.

**They care about what you do.**

# Too Much Planning, Too Little Execution

In the late 1990s, Kevin took on a consulting assignment to work with a large firm based in Japan. A U.S. division of the firm had been faltering, and management just seemed to be stuck, paralyzed in the downward spiral. The president was removed, and headquarters in Japan had asked Dick Rosen, chairman and former CEO of AVX Corporation, to step in for a couple of months to help get the company back on track.

Rosen is a stellar leader and a get-it-done kind of guy. The organization had suffered from what Patrick Lencioni calls "death by meeting." Shortly after his arrival, in an offsite retreat, Rosen had seen enough. In a fit of frustration he stood up in the middle of an executive's planning presentation and barked, "Look, you've got to stop planning and do something!" Obviously thrown by the interruption, the executive looked back and said, "Do what?" Rosen yelled,

"SOMETHING INSTEAD OF NOTHING!"

It was an instructive moment for Kevin, and we are sure it was an epiphany for the fifty executives in the room. Rosen's passion for execution and candor jolted the organization out of its slumber.

You cannot make a difference in neutral.

Great innovators have many things in common; chief among them is DSN. Not tomorrow, not next week or next month, but now. At the end of the journey, what ultimately determines the quality of your life, your value to your organization and your impact upon the world is what you do.

Faith without works is dead.

**This book is about making DSN part of your DNA.**

**Do you really want to be the person sitting around the party telling worn out stories about a great idea, that you had first—an idea that was implemented by, well...**

# someone else?

# So You Have An Idea...

What now? The only limitation to the creation and development of a new product or service, a better process or a radically different business model is your willingness to step up and give it a shot.

Sure, there are hurdles to overcome. You need political support, capital, time, talent, and expertise to pull it off. There's no free ride here. But if you are telling yourself that it can't be done you've hijacked the whole process before you've even had a chance to test the waters.

Beware of James Arthur Baldwin's famous words, *Those who say it can't be done are usually interrupted by others doing it.* Successful innovation has always been part exploration, part ideation and part perspiration and perseverance.

The challenge is to focus on the importance of the work, solving a problem that matters; not on what you lack or why you can't do it. Fear will always take you to those places. So you have to stand up to it and ask, *Do I believe in this enough to fight for it? Is my passion for finding a solution bigger than my fear?*

## Have you ever been in the position of seeing someone else execute on your idea?

It feels terrible, particularly when you look in the mirror and have no one to blame but yourself. Over the course of our careers several books have been written that we envisioned, but failed to pull the trigger on. They were really good books, written by great thought leaders. We are truly glad the content has changed people's lives and made the world better.

But, frustrated, foolish, and disappointed are just of a few of the words that come to mind when we think about the missed opportunity. Great ideas are wonderful, but they don't do the world a damn bit of good unless you take them to market. Perhaps you DID have the idea first, it really doesn't matter because the world rewards those who make things happen first.

## DESIRE + ACTION =
## What separates those who *do* from those who *don't*.

**One First Class Passenger to Another:**

**What do you do?**

**I'm the Chief Instigation Officer for our company.**

**What's that mean?**

**I make shit happen!**

# DSN is hard

## That's why it's so rare.

The scarcest resource in your organization right now is not money or talent or ideas or power; it's people who will DSN.

## Innovation is about lots of starts.
## Lots of starts means lots of mistakes.

Is this the right project or product? Will this marketing campaign succeed? If it does succeed what kind of ROI will it produce? Do we have the talent and resources to enter this market?

The answers to these questions don't come easily. If they did people would already be where you are going. Running with an idea or rejecting it requires rigorous analysis—and that's hard because we usually don't give risk a fair assessment.

When facing an uncertain opportunity to DSN our natural defense mechanism is to assume the worst and prepare to avoid the threat: *What could go wrong? What Am I losing? How bad will it hurt?*

Every time you start something risky, new or untried, you're vulnerable. You might do the wrong thing. Doing the wrong thing means you could be blamed, ostracized or rejected—and that feels bad.

This one-sided analysis almost always leads to self-protection, which will always suggest you should play it safe. The problem is that this biased risk assessment blinds us from seeing the upside of DSN: *What could go right? What am I gaining? How good will it feel?*

## Starters. Initiators. Doers.

These people are the exception to the rule which is why they are so valuable—and indispensable!

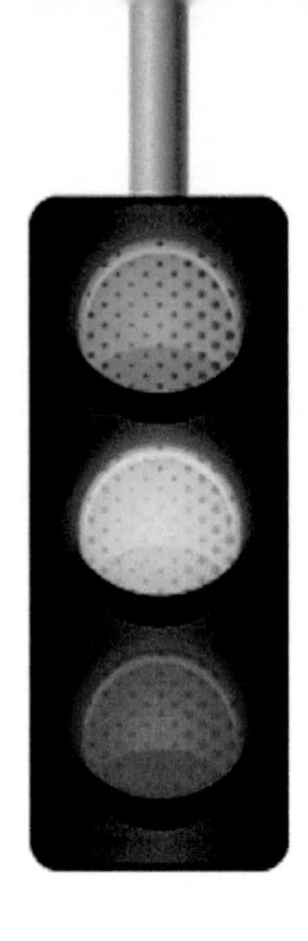

# Uncertain about...

who will support it........ ask
how it works........ play with it
the assumption........ question it
what's out there........ go find out
what it means........ do some research
how to make it better........
step up and try it
the timing........
NOW might be as good as any.

# Take Control

## Struggling with UNCERTAINTY?

When you're going 90 mph with your hair on fire in conditions that change constantly, you won't always have a complete picture. If the answers were clear and the data definitive, it would be easy to draw conclusions, make decisions and lead.

If the windows of opportunity stayed open just a little bit longer and the schedule wasn't so tight you could plan a more thorough attack. If the landscape of business wasn't so complex and politically charged, you could navigate more accurately and freely. "If, if, if, if only..."

Uncertainty makes all of us feel vulnerable—out of control. It seduces us to hunker down. Wait and see. Let things settle. Wait for the chaos to clear.

## But it never happens.

As former Intel CEO Andy Grove put it, *"None of us has a real understanding of where we are heading. But decisions don't wait for the picture to be clarified. So you take your shots and clean up the bad ones later."*

Just because you don't completely understand what's going on within your organization or in the market, that doesn't give you a license to take a seat on the sidelines.

Stop looking higher up the organizational chart for clarity and security. Don't wait for your boss or your boss's boss to step out of her office to slow everything down and explain your place in the crazy world of work. Don't play dumb and don't act like you don't know what needs to be done. Rally the people you need, go get the information you want, and DSN.

**Take control of uncertainty or it will take control of you!**

Uncertainty expands when you hunker down, so ask yourself, "How much of my uncertainty stems from my lack of initiative. What would happen if I started to move, to focus on the things I CAN control?"

## Dare to dream big. Then, engage!

**DSN probably means that you will end up in a place that's different
from where you originally intended to be.**

**If this uncertainty bothers you, you can play it safe and never get hurt. But then...**

**You will miss the adventure!**

# Give Uncertainty a Chance

## Are you sure?

We've heard the question most of our lives. It's a voice that rings in our head. It invites us to believe we should always be certain.

To move toward something for which the outcome cannot be assured is unsettling. We want life to be predictable, but we also want change and "predictable" doesn't usually go with change.

Uncertainty never really ends. If you choose the road of innovation, contribution, impact, and growth, rest assured that uncertainty, risk and exposure will almost always come with it.

## Here's another way to think about uncertainty.

It's an opportunity. Uncertainty upsets our equilibrium and rattles our cage, but this unfreezes our rigid ways of thinking and challenges our preconceived notions about the way things work.

Uncertainty makes us mentally flexible and more open to fresh, new ways of seeing the world. Uncertainty can open our eyes to new trends, and where these trends intersect there is opportunity.

This creates more dots to connect and unleashes a wave of ingenuity that creates more efficient processes, unique products and services and radically different business models that are hard to compete with.

We get it—the world is an uncertain place. The danger comes when you wallow in the confusion and discomfort uncertainty brings and fail to see it for the gift it offers.

## The pay-offs for personal growth and corporate ingenuity are greatest when uncertainty is the highest.

What if you stopped running from uncertainty and leaned into it? What if you came through it changed, stronger and better equipped to leverage the opportunities on the other side? What if this made your organization a stronger, more vibrant place to work?

**We Ain't No**

**...Face Savin,**

**...Excuse Makin,**

**...Rule Followin,**

**...Fun Squelchin,**

**...Permission Seekin,**

**...Status Quo Protectin,**

**Clock Punchin,**

**Bureaucrats**

**We're Risk Takers, Trail Blazers,**

**Rule Breakers and**

**Revolutionaries**

**WE MAKE A DIFFERENCE!**

# Initiator or Order-taker?

Most people are waiting for someone—usually with a C-Suite title—to tell them what to do. If THEY would just tell us what to do we could proceed. If THEY would just give us direction we could move. There THEY are again.

Is your organization really that short on people who know what to do? Our bet is that you have plenty of people who know what to do.

The true experts in most organizations are in the trenches, at the point of action. They see the waste and redundancy. They understand what turns customers on and off. They know the customers' pressure and pain points. And, they see the opportunity—for improvement, differentiation and growth.

**The true experts in any organization are those at the point of action.**

It's the new marketing guy who thinks, "If Starbucks, Google, Amazon, Southwest Airlines or GE ran our business what would they do." And then does it.

It's the receptionist who finds a better way to welcome clients or the call center person who gets to resolution in one call versus three—without sounding scripted or robotic. It's the sales person who sees an opportunity to leverage a core capability in a different industry and then creates a whole new revenue stream.

The problem in most organizations isn't people who don't know what to do; it's a shortage of people who are willing to DSN.

## DSN isn't something someone gives you—you take it.

The world doesn't need or want more order takers. It wants people who start things—like you.

If you're waiting for a set of directions, stop waiting and create your own. Yep, you might choose the wrong direction and that won't feel good, but you will most certainly be wrong standing still.

Do you want to build a reputation as a GO-TO person? Stop acting like you don't know what to do and start something. You will STAND OUT immediately.

If you don't have some fear or anxiety, the problem you're solving might not be big enough.

**Think Bigger!**

# Odds are There... to be Challenged

On May 25, 1961, President John F. Kennedy announced the dramatic and ambitious goal of putting an American on the moon and bringing him home safely before the end of the decade.

The dream was bold and audacious, but it galvanized a nation and launched a movement. That one simple, yet extraordinary declaration ignited the entire U.S. scientific community along with an army of government officials and private sector entrepreneurs. Thousands of people worked insanely long hours making personal and professional sacrifices to bring thousands of puzzle pieces together.

Everyday these pioneers got up and started something. And then, they restarted and started again. Eventually a rocket was launched that put a man on the moon. DSN is like that. You wake up and DSN over and over again until you launch—and then you land.

Experts estimate that we only knew approximately 15 percent of what we needed to know to accomplish this goal when Kennedy made the commitment. Yet somehow a critical mass of innovators and technologists opened their minds, tapped into the intellectual capital of the nation, and rose to the occasion.

Kennedy was the catalyst. He had a dream, but his dream was empowered by a start. Had it not been for his courage to DSN one of the greatest mobilizations of resources and manpower in history might never have happened.

## Great history lesson, but what's in it for you?

Well, what if there was a myriad of people, technologies and networks waiting to launch if only someone would put a stake in the ground and DSN? What if a world of resources and talent, ready to come to your aid, just needs a pilot light? What if you could improve one person's life or disrupt an entire industry if you chose to DSN?

## Are you brave enough to find out?

YOU only find oil if you drill wells. You may think you're finding it when you're drawing maps and studying logs, but you have to drill.

**John Masters**

Canadian Oil and Gas Wildcatter

# Ideas Won't Grow Your Business...Starting Will

Great ideas. They are the lifeblood of your organization and the key to your future. But here's the problem. Ideas don't start themselves. They require someone to DSN.

And here's the deal. Innovation tests the validity of an idea through trial and error. The faster you put your ideas out there, the faster you learn about what works and doesn't work.

DSN-learn-modify. DSN-learn-modify. This cycle can be a huge competitive advantage—but only if you're willing to start.

**Your business needs initiators who can convert great ideas into commercial success that is, relevant solutions people can't live without**

Think about it, the shelf life of your products and services keeps getting shorter and shorter. Too often incumbents, those who created yesterday's wiz-bang innovation, have a hard time letting go.

When the world is applauding you for what you did yesterday it's hard to start something new. If the goal is perpetual innovation the most important resource you have is starters— people who say YES to something new and then DSN!

## But this means you have to LET GO!

Action drives progress. Inertia—indolence, lethargy, and sluggishness—kills it.

This is what made Steve Jobs so remarkable, among many things. He was an initiator. In between letting go of yesterday's clunky iPod and creating tomorrow's iPod nano was a person, reputedly an impatient person, who perfected the "art of the start."

## Take action now and learn as you go.

A journey of a thousand miles begins with the first step.

**Host a summit...**
**Test a new prototype...**
**Accept a tricky challenge...**
**Jettison the daily routine...**
**Take the more dangerous route...**
**Stretch yourself for a noble, heroic cause...**

# Get UNstuck

Stuck in the same old job that's boring you to death? Stuck in a stagnant industry with a declining market? Stuck with colleagues who defend the same old product line and the same old distribution channel; unwilling to see that disintermediation is causing your demise?

Are you stuck in a routine? Stuck in your marriage? Stuck with friends who have little interest in meaningful conversation or in challenging themselves? Join the crowd. We don't know anyone who hasn't been stuck at one point or another.

## But breaking out involves some risk.

You have to risk more to gain more. If the truth be told, perception is often what kills initiative. The perception of stepping out is usually scarier than actually stepping out of the comfort zone.

Our brains immediately go to worst-case scenario and equate risk with failure. Stepping out triggers an automatic response: If I DSN it increases the chance that I will fail. Failure sucks because it usually means rejection, being wrong, looking foolish.

Your brain is right. If you DO step out you WILL increase the chance of failing. The more you try, the more mistakes you will make.

This is why starting is so hard.

## When you are sick and tired of being sick and tired—you DSN.

OKAY, so you've done a thorough analysis of what would happen if you DSN and fail. You've got that wired. But have you fully estimated the cost of doing nothing?

You know that thing you've been wanting to do? What if you did it? What if you just started—today, right now?

## What if it turned into great work—that matters?

**Okay, so you did nothing wrong. Maybe that's the problem... you did nothing wrong!**

**RISK MORE FAIL FASTER**

# Rethink Failure

If he misses 70 percent of the time, a baseball player is considered a good hitter. Want to innovate? Redefine failure.

Failure builds resilience, exposes blind spots, broadens your perspective, and moves you closer to a solution. Have no shame in ideas that don't work. Learning what doesn't work is as important as learning what does.

Eventually, BANG! you find a breakthrough and take one more step toward a more elegant solution.

Watch Michael Jordon on failure link: http://oqr.me/OSWUd

If you're waiting for a guarantee before you DSN, forget it. Innovation rejects proven solutions and offers you no guarantees. You say, "That makes me uncomfortable." We know. That's why most people fail to DSN and that's why organizations get stuck.

Most of the decisions you make are not life and death. So put on your big-girl panties and stop looking for who's in charge of YES.

From now on you're in charge.

# DSD

## (Do something different!)

**DSD = Unforgettable.**

**Unforgettable = category of one.**

**Category of One = define the rules of the game.**

**Rule Maker = competitors play catch up.**

## DSD demands DSN!

# Will You Be Missed?

If we were to jettison you, your department, business unit or company off the face of the earth, would you be missed?

Would there be weeping and gnashing of teeth on the part of your customers and clients because they couldn't get along without that unique, hard-to-replicate, thing you do?

Would they be begging for your return because of the unique value you add or contribution you make?

## Or…

Would a competitor who steps into the breach and fills the gap make it relatively seamless for the customer because they can do what you do and the difference between you, well…ISN'T?

## Not sure if you'd be missed?

Then come up with one good reason why you're not in jeopardy of losing customers.

**Your lock on success is only as good as your last piece of work.**

**No one is paying you today for what you did yesterday. When you stop bringing something new and fresh and exciting to the game...**

**...the game is over.**

# De-Commoditize It

Madonna. Lady Gaga. Steve Jobs. Richard Branson. Hummer. Mini Cooper. What do they have in common? They are unforgettably distinct.

We live in a world of clutter, a sea of sameness. In a "surplus society" where we have too many choices everything gets commoditized very quickly. From automobiles and appliances to hospitality and professional services, we are no longer impressed when things work right the first time. Everything works right the first time; if it doesn't it's gone. Getting it right only buys you an admission ticket to the game.

## What makes you unforgettable?

It's an important question because what makes you unforgettable makes your competitors uncomfortable.

What makes you...special? Special = distinct, unique, remarkable, indispensable, hard to emulate, one-of-a-kind.

## Does that describe you? Your business? Your life?

If yours really isn't any different than theirs and theirs is cheaper, people are gonna take theirs.

Does everyone in your professional service firm look and act like everyone in every other PSF? Is the design and quality of your car basically the same as theirs? Does your computer basically do for me what a hundred others will do for me? Is your burger pretty much the same as theirs?

In a sea of sameness it's not enough to be different; you have to be radically different. But that presents a problem. The minute you step out of the comfort zone and into the realm of the radical, someone is going to think you're nuts. Someone is going to tell you why you're not being a team player.

It takes courage to find that unique point of differentiation, that value proposition people can't live without. That's why so few people and businesses really stand out.

Here's the truth. You *are* unique, different, one-of-a-kind. You were created to bring something to the world no one else can bring the way you do. You're wired for success.

## So, quit trying to fit in and bring it!

**We have a strategic plan.**

**It's called**

# DOING THINGS!

**Herb Kelleher,**

**Founder and Chairman Emertus,**

**Southwest Airlines**

# Stop Waiting for Permission

If you are going to DSN you have to get rid of THEM.

## THEY are the ones who decide…

…if we'll be selected for that promotion, lead the team or run a project,

…if we will get our book published, song recorded or article reviewed,

…if we will be cast to play that role or get funding for that new idea.

THEY are the ones who give us permission—to think and act and share our ideas.

The problem is that THEY are often a figment of our imaginations. Frequently, we really don't even know who THEY are, but we know THEY are out there—making us wait, holding us back.

## And, as long as THEY are out there we have an excuse.

We have someone to blame for our reticence to act. Because of THEM we are not responsible. No more accountability, we're free!

## Or are we?

Putting your job satisfaction and ability to make a difference in the hands of others gives them the power to run your life. This doesn't sound much like freedom. Letting someone else decide the worthiness of your ideas and fate of your dreams and desires sounds like abdication not liberty. Where's the dignity in that?

Maybe, through our own free will we, unwittingly, become "prisoners of our thoughts." Maybe, we are the greatest enemy we face. Could it be that your real limits are out there somewhere beyond the ones you imagine?

## Maybe it's time to get rid of THEM and DSN!

Do you know someone who is waiting for permission? Send them this book with a note that says: Someone believes in you. They hired you because they think you are capable, you have what it takes. They've backed you because they believe in your ideas. And, they've equipped you because they're expecting you to DSN!

## "Damn the torpedoes, full speed ahead!"

# REWARD...

...Intelligent failure

...people who dare to try

...the ones who dare to be different

...those who question the unquestionable

# Good Stories Promote DSN

We don't live in a world that majors in catching people doing things right. If we did, more people would DSN. We live in a world that has perfected the "let's point out what didn't work and find somebody to blame" game.

Even though we recount the failures of Edison, Churchill, and Lincoln as badges of honor, the truth is we are preoccupied with pointing fingers at people who try big things and fail.

If you doubt this, do a content analysis of the local and national news for a month. Dissect the commentary of a ball game. Watch the ads of a political campaign (no don't do that). Or, review the marks your children bring home from school.

Why is the ratio of good stories to bad stories in the news so appalling? Are we really that bad? Do we really relish building ourselves up by putting others down?

In school, why is it always about how many we get wrong? Do we really believe the red marks encourage students to think big and act bold?

How many signs are we confronted with that tell us DON'T as in don't do this or that vs. DO? How often are we told YOU CAN'T vs. YOU CAN? Policy manuals, rules and bureaucracies are designed to contain, control and prevent. More often they throw a wet blanket on creativity.

## What would happen if we gave people fewer rules and majored in catching them doing things right?

Would we celebrate failure as an essential part of growth?
Would we attract the best candidates for the best jobs—including political jobs?
Would we build a community, organization, or nation of people who reach higher?
Would we unleash the power of initiative and accelerate the rate of innovation?

## What's it like to work with you?

Do you have a reputation for playing "gotcha" and adding another page to the policy manual or for rewarding intelligent failure? Have you contributed to a fear-based culture that stifles risk taking and initiative or a culture where people feel free to DSN?

**If you always play it safe, make the right decision and take the politically correct road, the one most people take, you will be like everyone else. Nice, but plain, predictable and boring...**

**...wishing you were**

# different.

# Zero Defects—Really?

If you want to find the true Sensei's of DSN go spend time with your children or grandchildren. They've got it down.

They role play, create things out of nothing, make up games, chew graham crackers into pistols, and then go take out the bad guys. They go from one adventure to the next—usually causing some kind of ruckus along the way leaving a trail behind.

They're masters at starting because they are open to the world and have few inhibitions. They don't care if they don't know. They've never been hammered for taking initiative. They've never been told their ideas are implausible. They've never had to stare into the disbelieving eyes of a CFO who holds the purse strings. And when they try something that doesn't work they forget about it and move on.

## Then they come to work for us.

Now because they are smart and learn very quickly our children, now adults (us) pick up on the rules for not being snubbed, scolded, ostracized, embarrassed, and rejected. They learn to compromise, optimize and synchronize.

They know we talk up heroes who exemplify rugged individualism, but we chastise nonconformity. We extol the virtues of commitment, but we reward compliance. We give speeches about risk taking, but require an inordinate number of signatures before people can act. It's a dysfunctional paradox.

## And it kills DSN.

They hear us say strong fish swim against the tide and weak ones with it. They hear us say we want creative contrarians who will push the edge of the envelope because that's the key to innovation, but secretly they know we are much more comfortable with command, control and convention. We criticize them for lack of initiative, but the unwritten rules governing the business (the ones that count) say do no wrong. It's a dysfunctional paradox.

## And it kills DSN.

Our ability to accelerate game-changing innovation is only as strong as our troublemakers, the irreverent few who refuse to be brainwashed by the culture. Is it time to encourage the troublemakers, reward those who stir the pot and rejuvenate the child-like spirit dormant in your organization?

# Only Those Who Dare To Lose WIN!

**What would you do today if you weren't afraid of...**

**making a mistake,
feeling rejected,
looking foolish,
or being alone?**

# What Makes You Tired?

Wishful thinking asks, Wouldn't it be nice if...? It usually takes you to woulda... coulda...shoulda—the project you envisioned, but never got around to or the life you wanted, but were never able to create. A wish satisfies. It takes you on a mental vacation from reality and gives you something fun to think about. But a wish is passive, not active. It will never hold you accountable and deliver the results you seek. DSN comes from being dissatisfied. It haunts you until you, well...DSN.

## DSN = going on offense—because you're agitated.

Tata Group Chairman, Ratan Tata saw families of four, five and six riding the same motorcycle at the same time and became agitated. He saw how unsafe it was. He witnessed the plight of these families riding their scooters in the monsoons and the blistering heat of the Indian summer. He knew that 100,000 fatalities occur every year in auto-related accidents—most of them on two-wheelers.

This was unacceptable. Agitation drove him to DSN. The day he unleashed his engineers to pursue a safe, affordable car that would cost slightly more ($2500) than the cost of a motorcycle is the day the (seemingly insurmountable) odds began to shift in his favor.

## DSN = going on offense—because you are tired.

On December 1, 1955, an African American woman, Rosa Parks, got on a Montgomery City bus to go home from work. She sat near the middle of the bus, right behind the seats reserved for whites. When a white man entered the bus and noticed that all of the seats were taken, the driver insisted that all four blacks give up their seats.

Mrs. Parks, quietly refused, was arrested, convicted and fined. On the day of her trial African Americans launched a boycott refusing to ride the buses until the U.S. Supreme Court ordered integration of public transportation one year later.

When she was asked why she didn't give up her seat, Rosa said, "I was tired." And let's be clear. It wasn't just her feet that were tired. Her one act ushered in a new era in the American quest for freedom and equality.

## What are you agitated about? What makes you tired? Is it enough to make you DSN?

**In life, most of us are highly skilled at suppressing action. All the improvisation teacher has to do is to reverse this skill and he creates very gifted improvisers. Bad improvisers block action, often with a high degree of skill. Good improvisers develop action.**

**Keith Johnstone, author of the classic: Improv for Storytellers**

---

**In making the film Jaws, Steven Spielberg said he was forced to improvise when the mechanical shark failed. He asked himself, "What would Hitchcock do?" The answer: "Hitchcock would never show the shark."**

# Improvise...
## But Leave Nothing To Chance

Thinking on your feet. Reacting and adapting to events you haven't planned for. Moving with lightning-quick speed to capitalize on market trends.

### This is the new normal.

And, it requires that you make important decisions on the fly. Improvisation techniques can teach us a lot about change and innovation because you can't be a successful improv comedian unless you DSN.

Improv is not as random and chaotic as you might think. It's an art form governed by a set of rules actors rehearse off-stage over and over again. A better way to characterize it might be "planned spontaneity." Here are the rules:

**Yes and**...no matter how radical or off-the-wall your idea or someone else's idea is, say "YES" and then add to it. Suspend judgment, see where it might take you.

**Go with Your Gut**...don't confuse appropriateness with fear. If you have a gut feeling that you are right, go for it.

**Be Open and Be Changed**...at any given moment, new information invites you to a new reaction or to experience a new facet of the scene.

Watch "Whose Line is it Anyway" link: http://oqr.me/KL8nD

**Co-create the Agenda**...the original agenda is abandon because there was no agenda, you co-create one—in real time. Someone starts and an agenda emerges.

**Mistakes are Invitations**...that invite actors into a new level of creativity. Performers feed off these expected, unexpected anomalies because they offer the element of surprise, shake up a scene taking it in new directions and make the audience laugh.

**Keep Moving**...regardless of what happens in a scene you accept it and keep the energy flowing. Unlike in business, where you stop to analyze, criticize and debate.

**Trust**...Each actor has to trust that the others are committed to making the scene work and moving the story forward. When everyone is committed to making their partner shine it frees the entire cast to experience a kind of creative combustion.

### The Musketeers got it right, "All for one and one for all!" The sum of the parts is greater than the whole.

# BRAND YOU...

It's not in your control. It's what your colleagues and customers say it is.

But you CAN influence it.

# BRAND = A PROMISE

It says, "Choose me and I'll make something happen."

Deliver on the promise and your brand equity goes up; if not it goes down.

## Delivering is about DSN.

# BRAND YOU...

It's yours to own.

# DSN Expands Your Resolve

DSN is an act of bravery that expands your influence and increases your leverage. It differentiates you and builds your reputation for being indispensable.

Courage takes practice. Practice comes from putting yourself in challenging situations that activate fear. That means, in order to exercise courage, you must be afraid. Like snake charmers who inoculate themselves—a little bit at a time—from the deadly effects of poison, courageous people develop self-confidence by taking risks, a little bit at a time.

When speaking up here, taking on a new assignment there, showing up in life more audaciously forces you to risk embarrassment, be afraid and act anyway.

Put yourself in enough of these challenging or dangerous situations and the strength of your resolve will grow over time. Then, starting and finishing things becomes a core capability.

Motion by the way, sets off a chain reaction. You start to connect with like-minded people interested in the same thing, going in the same direction. You notice things, resources, opportunities and ideas that you would not have noticed had you not started moving.

DSN has a magnetic effect. You start and the next steps appear. Solutions emerge. Answers come to you. Unseen resources rally to your aid. The way becomes more clear. Your momentum picks up speed and eventually something good happens.

**The more things you try, the more you get better at trying things.**

Richard Branson has built a $4 billion enterprise structured around 200 small companies. Branson is the poster child for DSN. He has created an organization characterized by perpetual motion.

Branson rarely says "No." Why? He loves to start things. People in his companies don't get stagnant because their ideas don't get lost; they get acted upon on—now!

And, as your bandwidth for action begins to grow your "try it: innovation" ratio grows as well.

**If you're not living on the edge, you're taking up too much space!**

# Step Through Fear

If you're going to DSN you have to learn to step through fear. No one is exempt from fear! It's not the absence of fear that enables you to DSN, it is your ability to step through fear that makes the difference.

Every time you choose to face fear and step through it, fear loses its grip. But if you cave into it, like a shark attracted to blood from a mile away, it can eat you alive.

## Ironically, fear is challenged through DSN.

You've probably seen the acronym F.E.A.R. (False Evidence Appearing Real). If you're going to bear down on it you have to call its bluff, you have to take charge of your thoughts by asking:

> Is the threat real—what is the probability that this will actually happen?
>
> Is everything I'm telling myself about this risk true? (Just because you believe it doesn't make it true.) How much valid evidence is there to support my fear?
>
> If what I fear comes to pass, how bad can it be? What's the worst-case scenario?
>
> Assuming the worst-case scenario, would I be able to cope with the consequences? What is the probability that I will be able to say, "So what?" and move on?
>
> How will my life, career, and company be positively impacted if I DSN? How will these things be negatively impacted if I do nothing? Will I be okay with this?

## Fear is the enemy. Guess what the enemy fears most? DSN!

Here are Kevin's insights on "stepping Through Fear"

## DSN = more opportunities to...

...step through fear, each time putting another weld on the bar of courage,

...claim your gifts and talents, each time developing and honing them into something more powerful,

...expand your tolerance for uncertainty and ambiguity, each time helping you see that you are more capable of change than you ever dreamed,

...increase your potential, each time putting more distance between you and your boundaries.

# DSN Is Contagious

When you act, you have the potential to stimulate action in others.

## Consider this simple scenario.

You pull up to an intersection behind a car that is stalled. Embarrassed because he or she is holding up traffic, the driver doesn't quite know what to do. All of the sudden another driver pulls over, jumps out of the car and begins to push the stalled car. Then another driver does the same thing. Pretty soon a cadre of people create enough momentum to push the car out of the way and traffic is moving again. The action of one person primed the pump for others to join in.

One person with the courage to speak up in a meeting often gives several others the courage to do the same. Action has the potential to impassion others. The courageous step you take today might be a gift to someone who is inspired to take bold action tomorrow.

Watch an example of this principal from "Lead India" link: http://oqr.me/OemVv

If you inspire enough people, your action could be the impetus for creating a YES-FAST culture—a culture that enables the organization to move with speed, agility and "adaptiveness."

People want leadership. You might be surprised at how many people would follow you if you would just lead the way and DSN.

## Enthusiasm breeds enthusiasm. Get excited!

**We are defined by the causes we serve and the problems we seek to solve.**

**Daring**
**Weighty**
**Soul-Stirring**
**Jaw-Dropping**

**Does this describe the cause for which you fight?**

# Find A Cause

## The pilot light for DSN gets lit with work that matters.

DSN springboards from doing something worth doing. Change is initiated by finding something worth changing for.

DSN isn't about order taking, doing what you are told to do or playing follow-the-leader; it's about NOTICING. You see a gap, decide the problem is worth solving, step into the breach, and fill the void. You get tired—tired of seeing the same old broken something abuse people you care about—so you act.

DSN is a response to a cause or calling. It's about believing in something so deeply that your work becomes a crusade. Game-changing innovation doesn't come from compliance. It comes from 100 percent, full-blown commitment.

## Compliance is about buy-in.

Buy-in happens when senior executives decide: *This is what we are going to do. Now, how do we get the people who have to execute on it to buy into it?* Compliance works—at least for a while. But it doesn't inspire the creativity and discretionary effort that leads to game-changing innovation.

## Commitment is about opt-in.

Opt-in happens when people are inspired by the bigness of the dream and the nobility of the cause it serves. Their response is: How can I play? I want in!

When the business becomes a cause, what follows is a movement. And here's the thing about movements. People do not need to be convinced; they can see themselves fighting for the cause, having a role in the movement. They do not need to be motivated; they motivate themselves. They do not need to be micro-managed; they set their own rigorous targets. They do not need to be told to collaborate; they willingly reach across boundaries because their passion for fulfilling the dream is bigger than their need to control information, turf, or other people.

## What is it in your life that will pull you out of your seat to do something extraordinary?

A good battle plan that you can act on today can be better than a perfect one tomorrow.

- General George Patton

How many tomorrows do you really have? What if tomorrow begins today?

# Stop Getting Ready

*We need more data. Let's research this further and meet next week. It's a great idea, but the timing is just not right, we could be too far in front of the curve. I don't think the market is ready for it yet.*

DSN isn't about planning to plan to do something. It's not about, *"Interesting idea, let's put a date on the calendar and talk about it?"*

Too many of us try to perfect something before we launch and that leads to tomorrow. You might create the best proposal, pitch or Power Point deck in the world. But if the world beats you to the punch it doesn't matter—you're late to the party. And now you're playing catch up.

Being right and being late won't help you become indispensable, and it won't help your organization achieve competitive advantage. We're talking about the kind of preparation people hide behind because they are afraid to act—where the cost-benefit analysis becomes a way of life. "We need to study it further" often becomes an excuse.

## What's wrong with NOW?

Instead of whittling on it until you reach perfection, run with what you've got and fix it as you go. Instead of holding back because you don't have enough hard proof that your idea will work, jump in, realizing that innovation rarely shows up in a tight, neat, step-by-step plan—and it isn't going to offer you any guarantees.

Forget the idea that you can have all the resources in place and know what is around every corner before you start. DSN requires a leap of faith that the necessary ingredients will be there.

## DSN = TNT (Today Not Tomorrow)

We're not talking about a blind leap of faith here. We're not coaxing you to do something reckless or impulsive. We're not asking you to gamble without a well-thought-out strategy. We're asking you to stop putting it off until tomorrow.

Do your homework. Rigorously prepare. Make sure you have the time, talent and resources to give it a great shot. Establish a strong business case for what you want to do, but don't get bogged down in perfection.

## Knowledge isn't power until you DSN.

# Destructive Content

**Satisfied with Being Dissatisfied =**

**Complacency...Mediocrity...Irrelevance**

# Constructive Discontent

**Dissatisfied with Being Satisfied =**

**3 X Better Tomorrow**

# It's Your Choice!

# DSN...Three Simple Letters

But place them side by side and they have the potential to transform companies, communities and nations.

In the world there are dreamers and doers. Exciting new ideas are the lifeblood of your business. They often come from the dreamers. But you also need people who can turn those ideas into solutions other people will buy—doers.

## Dreamers and doers.

We must have both, but there is a shortage of doers. So what are you going to do?

Are you going to keep dreaming about what you should be doing or are you going to do something about what you've been dreaming?

Are you going to point out the problem and say, "Somebody should do something about that?" Or are you going to roll up your sleeves and say...

## "I'm somebody!"

Here's the thing. Identifying the problem and dreaming about its solution is a great way to get things started. But DSN is the only way to get things done.

Great change efforts. Product innovations. Industry disrupting business models. And the process improvements in your company that enable you to sleep better at night started with someone who had the nerve to DSN!

Are you really happy with the status quo? Have you really become satisfied with your current skill set? How much shelf-life do you think your products and services really have? Are you really different from your competitors or are you becoming commoditized?

If you are willing to tell the truth, then you know there is an incredible future waiting to be created and what it needs is someone—like you—to...

## DSN!

Success is journey, not a destination. Remain happily discontent.

## Stay hungry. Stay foolish.

Those who lack
the courage to

**DSN**

will always find a
way to justify it.

# What's Your Nail?

You may have heard the story about the farmer sitting on his front porch with an old Bloodhound at his feet, moaning.

A visitor came by to chat and noticed the hound groaning. The visitor asked the farmer,

*What's wrong with the hound?*

*He's sittin' on a nail.*

*Why doesn't he move?*

*I guess it just doesn't hurt bad enough.*

Too often we would rather live with the comfort of the status quo—however boring or painful or dysfunctional it may be—and complain about it rather than do something risky and change it.

## What's your nail?

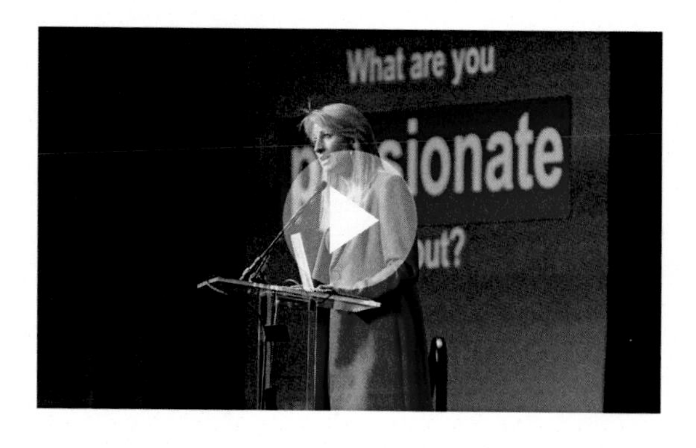

Jackie's question, "What's Your Nail?" will challenge you to look in the mirror."

Your organization is looking for people who are looking—people who want more, who want to reach higher and are willing to *DO SOMETHING* about it.

Your world is looking for people who want to MOVE; not MOAN.

## KEY TO YOUR SUCCESS...

DECIDE WHAT IT IS YOU WANT.
WRITE THAT SHIT DOWN.
MAKE A PLAN.
AND . . .
WORK ON IT.
EVERY.
SINGLE.
DAY.

# Stay started

When it comes to…

…selling your idea,

… promoting your product,

… rallying others,

… growing your business, and

… building your brand

here's what our friend Brig Hart says about gaining acceptance:

## SWSWSWSW: Some Will. Some Won't. So What? Some Will!

You will always run into the cynics, soothsayers and those who tell you why it won't work, why it's not for them or why it's too difficult.

But you get to choose whether or not you are going to let other people decide how you are going to act.

When you are pursing something daring and difficult the temptation to get distracted will be powerful and persistent.

But you get to choose whether or not you are going to let those distractions dilute your focus and derail you.

Just because you START doesn't mean the demons of doubt won't start talking in your head.

But you get to choose whether or not you will listen to them or recognize them for what they are and shut'em down.

We've already said it, "Starting is hard." If you quit you have to start all over again.

Stay started.

# DSN is about...

**instigating, insisting,**

**initiating...**

**pushing, prodding,**

**cajoling...**

**stirring, starting,**

**stimulating...**

# What Your Business Needs...

It needs people who are willing to trade hope for action. Hope is necessary, but it's not a strategy. Your business doesn't need people who hope for the best and hunker down to prepare for the worst. It needs people who are hungry for change.

It needs gutsy leaders who have the chutzpah to undo unnecessary rules. Undo command and control. Undo cheap talk. Undo hypocrisy. Undo outdated assumptions. Undo gender, generational and geographical prejudices. Undo me-too products and services.

It needs passionate, fearless people who believe that leadership is not a title or position; but a choice. It needs leaders—at every level—who prefer the adventure of stepping into the breach over the security of sitting on the sidelines.

It needs people who prefer to fold back that "accusing finger and clench it into a determined fist." People who desire to be part of the solution instead of being part of the problem.

## If you ran your company...

Would you do something about the broken processes and dysfunctional systems that frustrate you and make it hard for customers to do business with you?

Would you ensure that discomforting information isn't ignored or rationalized away as it moves up the hierarchy? Would you encourage the restlessly curious to levy their wacky ideas in order to find the next breakthrough?

**There is no good time to get started. So now is as good of time as any.**

**Brig Hart,**
**Best-selling Author,**
***Why Not You? Why Not Now?***

Would you create a culture that refuses to bask in the glory of yesterday's headlines and daydream about the future—a culture where action-oriented people, like you, are continually loading the pipeline with fresh ideas that become NEXT practices?

## Well, really, who's stopping you?

Maybe NOW is the time to put this book down and go DO that thing you've been thinking about.

# Theodore Roosevelt

## 26th President of the United States

It's not the critic who counts, not the man who points out how the strong man stumbled, or when the doer of deeds could have done better. The credit belongs to the man who is actually in the arena; whose face is marred by dust and sweat and blood; who strives valiantly; who errs and comes short again and again; who knows the great enthusiasms, the great devotions and spends himself
in a worthy cause; who at the best, knows in the end the triumph of high achievement; and who at the worst if he fails, at least fails while daring greatly, so that his place shall never be with those cold and timid souls who know neither victory or defeat.

Translation:

**DO SOMETHING NOW!**

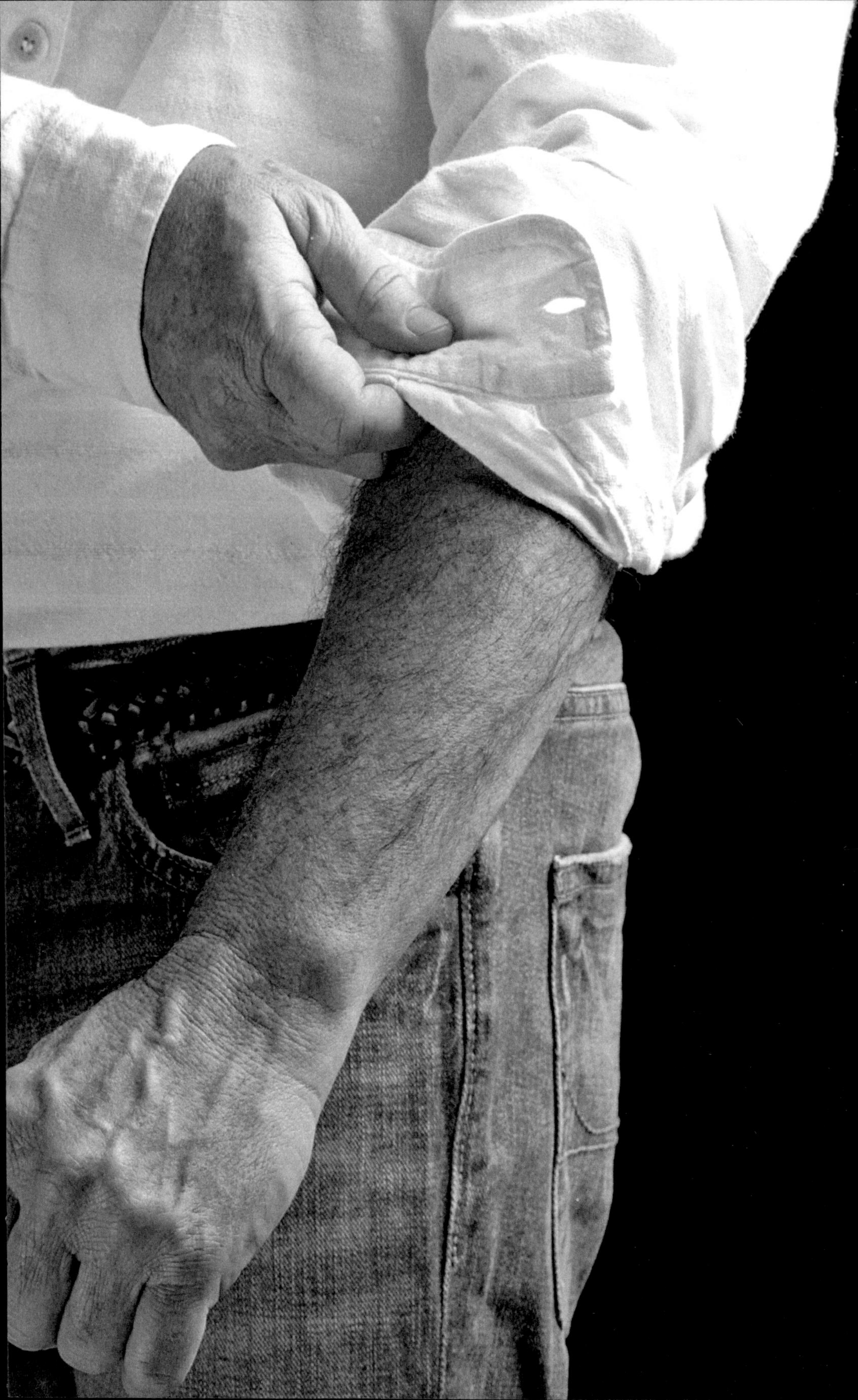

# Jackie and Kevin Freiberg

Are bestselling authors and founders of the San Diego Consulting group, a firm dedicated to equipping leaders for a world of change. Both Ph.D.s, they have taught at the University of San Diego's School of Leadership and Education Sciences.

In their international bestseller NUTS! Southwest Airlines Crazy Recipe for Business and Personal Success, Kevin and Jackie uncovered the strategies that created the greatest success story in the history of commercial aviation. NUTS! was followed by GUTS: Companies that Blow the Doors Off Business-as-usual and BOOM! 7 Choices for Blowing the Doors Off Business-as-usual.

Their most recent book, NANOVATION: How a Little Car Can Teach the World to Think Big, is the inside story of one of the greatest innovations in the auto industry since the Model-T. It's also a roadmap for expanding your capacity to innovate and making innovation part of your cultural DNA.

The Freibergs lead innovation seminars all over the world. They have a global practice including firms in Europe, Japan, India, South Africa, Central and South America, as well as companies throughout the United States and Canada.

We want to hear from you at kevinandjackie@freibergs.com

in/jackiefreiberg

in/kevinfreiberg

drjackie/2freibergscom/

kevinandjackie

For multiple copies and bulk orders, please contact our office

**T: 619.624.9691 / E: info@freibergs.com**